The Scientist's Wife

poems by

Miriam Flock

Finishing Line Press
Georgetown, Kentucky

The Scientist's Wife

Copyright © 2021 by Miriam Flock
ISBN 978-1-64662-616-8 First Edition
All rights reserved under International and Pan-American Copyright Conventions. No part of this book may be reproduced in any manner whatsoever without written permission from the publisher, except in the case of brief quotations embodied in critical articles and reviews.

ACKNOWLEDGMENTS

Chicago Review, "From the Dark Lady V, VI"
Cumberland Review, "The Scientist's Wife," "Proprioception"
Georgia Review, "From the Dark Lady I, II, III, IV, VII"
New Ohio Review, "Chickens in Your Backyard"
Poetry, "If Ontogeny Does Not Recapitulate Phylogeny, Then What Is Metaphor?"
Salmagundi, "Fight or Flight"
Santa Clara Review, "Drafting"
Shenandoah, "Lily in the House"
Southwest Review, "Homebody"

My deepest gratitude to Michael J. Rosen, my constant reader.

Publisher: Leah Huete de Maines
Editor: Christen Kincaid
Cover Art and Design: Michael J. Rosen
Author Photo: Howard Schulman

Order online: www.finishinglinepress.com
also available on amazon.com

Author inquiries and mail orders:
Finishing Line Press
PO Box 1626
Georgetown, Kentucky 40324
USA

Table of Contents

From the Dark Lady 1

Drafting 5

The Scientist's Wife 6

Lily in the House 8

Corollaries 9

Fight or Flight 10

Chickens in Your Backyard 11

Proprioception 12

If Ontogeny Does Not Recapitulate Phylogeny, Then What Is

    Metaphor? 13

Superwoman Awakens 14

He Wants Another Child 15

She Refuses to Move 16

Bosom Friend 17

Homebody 19

Happy Ending 20

To my husband, Howard Schulman, who is a scientist but definitely not the *scientist.*

From the Dark Lady

I.
What I might be like in the other room
is what I am like sipping the sauterne,
only not quite as sweet. Observe my jaw,
its angle: so my shoulders would be square.
My hair, if freed from this chignon, would rush
to cover them. Are you imagining
that, as it spills, I might seem less severe?
You can, from my dark brows and olive skin,
extrapolate the color of my breasts.
You know I won't be subtle; you know, looking
at my legs (the patch that shows above the boot)
that I am built for the fields. My calves would feel
like packed earth. This must be what you want.
You know I'll never be more beautiful.

II.
After the mannish blazer and the boots,
the bedclothes took you by surprise; their frills—
the quilt's trapunto and the lace-trimmed slips—
a sentimental touch, like sampler verse.
Tomorrow, waking in these fripperies,
you may read something different in the sheets:
This is a woman's bed; if she desires,
its pastel shams will frame your bearded face.
At that, you're better off than she, sleepless
and chilled by drying sweat. She watches you
as though across a clean white field of snow,
detecting in the fallen comforter
the evidence of how she took you in
her bed, her body, her uncovered life.

III.
How monkish your apartment and how still
after our bodies' twining filigree,
the canticle of our delight. You doze,
I stare the long way from this pallet up
to heaven. Though I haven't prayed in years,
imagined that odd snatch of angel talk
Moses overheard, I say it now.
The words intrude my God into your bed.
With my mouth tasting of your mouth, I add
your name to those I pester Him to bless.
Now in your dreams, the pomegranate tree
will bring forth fruit, the rose of Sharon bloom,
and a gazelle will call you in my voice:
Arise, Beloved, fair one, come away.

IV.
The argument we had, I should have had
with my last lover. Because you wanted me,
as he had, when I wore this flannel shirt,
I saw him toss the cloth across the lamp,
and in the green glow, close over me.
But mostly, I recalled he didn't love
the way my hair held smoke; that once I gripped
his back so hard, the skin striped red and white;
the way I couldn't let things go. Tonight
I couldn't; you were right. I was afraid
to be undone. Someday I'll let you touch
my heart, not just its place beneath the plaid,
or with my own hands tear the buttons free;
and let that be my argument with him.

V.
At ten a voice—not yours—hymns in the street,
"Amazing Grace." The neighbor scrapes a chair.
Later a bike, wheels ticking as it slows,
rounds the corner and fades out toward the bridge.
The wind chimes imitate your keys; the wind,
I'd swear, is the soft yielding of the lock.
But when you do arrive, no other sound
could match your entrance. From the bed I hear
the suck of boot sole on linoleum,
your leather jacket slap the leather chair.
I know what drawers you open, what you leave
as clutter: biscuits, mail, a sodden towel.
I know, from the impatience of your step
along the hall, you still won't let me sleep.

VI.
Your wet chest rises over me, as slick
and treacherous as stone. Groping for niches—
the blade, the clavicle, the lower back—
I rise, and then slip down, and rise again,
until the summit is beyond believing.
From here, whatever lies over the edge
looks hard, so dizzying—the smell of sweat
or sea—I can't remember how to move.
If you would teach me this terrain, to grasp
your body as a rope—an arm to brace
my arm, a leg to pass beneath my thigh—
I could come down rappelling, understand
the echo in that word: to recollect;
to muster, as in courage; to call back.

VII.
You thought that darkness was, like absence, something
missing—the cleft between, the space inside.
But I could show you substance to the dark
insides of mouths, a gravity to eyes
so dense they swallow light like lumps of jet.
This darkness has the mass and warmth of hips
beneath an army blanket—hills at dusk,
not green, not any color, giving back
the day's heat. Before your iris opens,
the dark you take in will assume these shapes:
my breasts, brown pears weighed in your upturned palms;
my head, a black cat sleeping on your chest;
my legs, dark swans that bill and glide apart;
my body, darkness that surrounds the dark.

Drafting

On our honeymoon, he taught me to ride
behind him, my bike hugging the sheer face
of the hill where it was hollowed to hold us.

In his wake, the way was easier, less prey
to the suction of trucks, through each still shook me
like an angry mother before its hold loosened.

Had I expected freedom in the slipstream—
that cave of air the windbreak of his body
fashioned for me? No, I was drawn to him

as though into an orbit. Drafting he called it,
and I thought of something provisional, a suggestion
for how we might be together. When I unfastened

my eyes from the road, the lake we had come to see
flashed in the intervals between rigs,
dull green through the revolution of his wheels.

The Scientist's Wife

> *All Nature is but art, unknown to thee.*
> —Pope

Elute is one of his words that won't stay with me,
except its beauty, but then, proofreading his text
(where I spot errors in parallel construction
without comprehending the sentence that contains them)
I see something is being purified, and I remember
how he extracts what he wants from what he doesn't.

If only I could comprehend what he must know
about my nature: not just my every caprice,
scampering down the nerves, branched like lightning,
but the second messengers, conveying the next step
I have only imagined across the fine membranes
that hold my cells together and apart.

Once, another woman captivated by his gift
for translating the unruly into formulas,
disrupted his dinner party disquisition to demand,
"What is the molecular mechanism of remorse?"
Immediately he began defining the problem: What happened,
what might have happened, the longing in between.

Though he cited the primitive state of his discipline,
I knew he believed only time could separate us
from the day shame would collect, an unmistakable residue
on a gel. Eventually he might track it to the very atom,
with valence itself a kind of yearning to unite
a different way. Everything in the physical world,

when he explains it, couples and uncouples, but inside
a single organism as though the world were self-contained
like he is. Even so conjugal a feeling as regret
would be resolved within his person, the body so populous
(with its insistently distinct mitochondria) that imagining another
is replaced by the more easily explainable

red of blood rising in the embarrassed cheeks.
In the last analysis what should he be sorry for?
While he may relish the random firings of desire,
the impulse never leaps the breach from thought
to trespass, and he loves everything he knows
about my nature, just not the art in it.

Lily in the House

In the yard, the bloom is everything
we hoped for: a black dragon. We ignore
the flicked tongue of pistil, snip the stem.
Too grand for our arrangements, she demands
to be alone and lolls in a blown glass bowl
dominating the dinner conversation.
The consommé is flavored with tarragon—
and lily. Oh, what drug is in the wine!
We breathe heavily but find ourselves
the next dawn, on the covers, fully clothed.
In spite, we relegate her to the den
and try to eat toast. For all our pains,
the house is thick with cheap perfume. At night,
after we bury her, we don't make love.

Corollaries

> *Let us look again at the laws of thermodynamics. It is true that at first sight they read like the notice at the gate of Dante's Hell.*
> —James E. Lovelock

Despite desire, a man can take a word back
only as he might a playing card
an indulgent opponent lets him return to his hand
though she has seen and even wanted his heart.

He may try to describe as inexorable the force
of attraction between their bodies, but choice
is his, if not what eddies from it, like plunging
a stick in the creek, altering the whorls.

And when he wants to recant brushing his lover's hair
one hundred strokes back from her face, while I apply
mascara in front of my childhood vanity,
there's no returning to the bridal bed.

Even if I couldn't see through the single rose
he buys from the back of a van on his way home,
he has changed everything. Time's not the river
hewing to its course (that would imply

the wrongs can be left behind) but water will do
for a metaphor. Imagine a still pool, halved
by a wall, the water on one side tinted red.
Now lift the barrier. In your mind, you do this

without turbulence. Still the dye will seep
into the plain side until the whole is stained
an even rose. Then, no matter how you wait,
the water won't unravel or clear again.

Fight or Flight

I.
What holds a heart? Tethered by veins, the muscle
clatters back against the pole of spine
like the ball in the old game. Biology
as fate. Perhaps he had been wiser in this,
defining both heart and bone as variants
of the same matter. And the mind, not hovering
as she'd envisioned it—something that floats
toward the white light of God—but indwelling,
indistinguishable from the mortal coil
of DNA. How else to explain
the fibrillation as his wayward hands
sought out the ordinary contour of her breasts
if not as random stimuli, a rain
of hormones over the dendritic tree?

II.
But she was not the wild deer she remembered
from a gravure in her grade-school science text.
Beneath its breast, she almost saw the heart
trying to rise, and in the widened eyes,
both hunter and the refuge of the pines.
Where it made tracks, she stood her ground,
turning to account her bounding pulse,
the breaths too fast to be deliberate.
Facing him now, she thought she recognized
the Bible's angel, a man to grapple with.
If she prevailed, she might have nothing more
than a new name, or she might find freedom
inside the urgings of adrenaline.
Fight or flight? She made her choice.

Chickens in Your Backyard

They come, like the dishwasher, with the house.
"No trouble," swears the seller, and—presto change-o—
for handfuls of Layena every morning,
the pair of hens trade one or two brown eggs.
The chick, if we approach with proper coos,
will let itself be stroked. This we learned
from our new bible, *Chickens in Your Backyard*.
Like neighbors of a different faith, we practice
tolerance, let them grub among the bulbs,
ignore the way their droppings singe the mulch.

Meanwhile, we are intent on our own nesting.
My husband paints the nursery; I quilt
a golden goose with pockets shaped like eggs.
We hardly register the added squawking
from the coop or look for more than tribute
when we rob the nesting boxes. Then
one dawn, I'm roused by what can only be
a cock-a-doodle-doo. And in the breaking light,
our chick-turned-rooster struts, ruffed as Raleigh,
shaking his noble scarlet comb. What waits

inside me to astonish like this male?
Such sudden majesty, sudden red.

Proprioception

> *It is only by the courtesy of proprioception, so to speak, that we feel our bodies as proper to us, as our property, as our own.*
> —Oliver Sacks

Ignoring my husband's bookish worry
that I might smother the baby in sleep,
I put my son to nurse and drift.

Whatever aura surrounds my body
must now extend to him, a glow
beyond the yellow of the bed light.

Something keeps us turning together,
as, barely awake, I break the seal
of breast and lips, shifting him.

All the peculiar kicks and jabs
by which I knew him before birth,
he now repeats like an escapee

from the silvered side of the mirror.
For nine months he redefined my borders
daily, as my growing form

grazed the desk, my husband's torso,
and the message from my skin
came back disorienting, distorted,

a signal that had moved through water.
When I had to remove my ring, I had faith
a self retained the old proportions,

simply waiting to be reclaimed.
But now I am this body, new,
between the sleepers I belong to.

If Ontogeny Does Not Recapitulate Phylogeny, Then What Is Metaphor?

So, those embryonic clefts aren't gills;
the coccygeal somites—no tail; the shushing
that overwhelms us through the stethoscope
is not the sea as we claim to hear it
in a chambered nautilus; and birth
is not the lungfish gasping on dry land.
Nothing is anything else, if you mean law:
a circle emerging from its formula.
Still, the baby has evolved from us,
not just his eyes—flecks of your blue,
flecks of my brown; not just the prehensile attack
on the breakfast cereal; but as he pulls to stand:
Homo erectus creating himself with the reach
that must exceed our grasp to make a metaphor.

Superwoman Awakens

This morning, my right arm has disappeared.
Is it sleeping or have I evolved
into elastic, just like Mr. Fantastic?
Rousing my husband, I'm Beast; my outsize feet
clatter over the floorboards. Before I fight
the Evil Twins of indolence and rage,
I must ingest the magic caffeine serum.
My husband has taken the news. I turn to ice,
my ring's enchantment fading. The Hulk in the mirror
strains at her buttons. The baby's morning feast
of pablum enervates like kryptonite.
Before this day is over, I will bend
the iron of my will with my bare hands.

He Wants Another Child

When he made love to her, she wasn't filled
with longing, but with the memory of herself:
The darkened skin of the *linea nigra*
split her belly like string on a brown parcel
she'd had to lug not knowing what she carried.

While the fetus fought that packaging,
she'd felt each flutter as the pulse of fear,
imagining the baby joining them
in flesh as they, unendingly, were joined
by the bursts and pauses of the argument

that was their marriage. She'd been wrong about that
and the son who was not like anyone.
"Good genes," he'd say when, with a precocious twist,
the baby's fingers wound the music box
or his fresh voice saluted his father's return

from hours at the microscope and the world
of blind experiments he never shared.
This faith in nature, she could recognize
as dangerous. She, too, found language early.
But what about her clumsiness, the flawed heart

she waited to inherit from her mother?
What about the fact he hardly spoke
except to ask for something? So much wrong
was incubating in them, she couldn't swear
that this time she would not give birth to it.

She Refuses to Move

These walls and all that stood between them
might, he insisted, be causing the friction:
the door punishing the jamb;
traffic patterns on the rug;
the nicked sash where the porch swing
banged the window frame, exposing
layers of trouble. The simple fact
of space, he claimed, could calm them,
as if they were no more than particles,
bombarded by the beautiful objects
they owned into a Brownian frenzy.
Move the baby from their room;
his cries would cease to wake them, silenced
like the tree in the deserted forest.
Blame the structure of the house:
the built-in plinth that dictated
the lofty placement of their bed
as though their joy were a facsimile,
like tombs of the Etruscans, connubial
even in death. Could an arrangement
confine the riot of their lives,
the child's splay of crumbs, of toys
diddled with and dropped, their own
raised voices? A house, she countered,
could only mediate between
perfection and what they could afford,
what concrete might be coaxed to do.
Even the vacant lot they paced,
delineating family room
and separate studies, contained its promise
within the frame of compromise:
so many by so many square feet,
where at their every measured footfall,
the muffs of dandelions quaked,
belying their intransigent roots.

Bosom Friend

I. In Arrivals
"Too long," we say in unison,
and clasp each other, bosom to bosom.
The flowers you hold out to me
are bread-and-butter gift or emblem
of desire. In the scarlet roses,
I could interpret an eleventh hour
detour to the airport florist or
some other brand of urgency.
All your gestures read two ways,
as if you were a teenaged boy
whose arm had strayed behind my back
in a darkened movie house.
Your woman's leg against my leg,
as we head north toward bay and vine,
might aim for nothing more than ease.
My husband's thigh against my thigh
feels much the same—a body, bared,
sticking to my pliant skin.

II. Tasting Room
My husband, who has done his share of tasting,
never likes more than a hint of the barrel;
it reminds him too much of decay.
But you detect a note of clove and smoke,
and for the first time, I believe I share
the tang that someone else is tasting.
Do our bodies' similarity
bring us closer to savoring the world
in the same way? Beneath both of our shirts,
the nipples rise and harden in the gust
from the open door. I'm tired of being alone
with myself. If I licked your tongue, purple
with wine, would I know it from my own?

III. Off the Beaten Track
This little vineyard has a following
among the cognoscenti, but Belle Helene
is not for tourists. So it is with passion,
you warn, between women. I cannot visit
as I might a summer house. This love
is like the vintner's field, green and golden
by turns, as I could only know, giving
myself up to it in every season.

IV. Jenner
Where the Russian River meets the sea
in a nebula of blue and white,
we troll Goat Beach for souvenirs
of two antagonists, however briefly,
kissing. In the hollow where your boots
emboss the sand, a single wandering tattler
reminds me of my little one, toddling.
We have to go back, take up our happy lives,
which are only happy at a distance.
This I see, facing the estuary,
where a pair of river hawks have strayed,
testing the sea before they circle home.

Homebody

For the gods of home, the Romans had the name
Penates, swelling from the root word *penus*,
not the garden Priapus you're picturing
with his improbable member, but where we enter—
storehouse, penetralia, the innermost parts.
Home is a woman's body. My body,
mortised to join with yours, tongue and groove,
anoints me genius of the place; you priest.
Yes, I admit we're corporate, heart and hearth
cemented through the body, however hard
we try to find, in art or even science,
a less homely truth. What if we've strayed
from the stolidity of our own door? It opens
to us still, and I want to be home.

Happy Ending

> *The Happy Ending Problem was a puzzle proposed by mathematician Esther Klein in 1933. She never solved it, but the problem got its name because, in the course of working on it, Klein fell in love with her future husband, George Szekeres.*

We have lasted like a problem
in arithmetic, two
known quantities, aligned
and added to each other, yielding

a remainder of love that carries over
to the next place. I sometimes wonder
if those who know us from the outside
see only the congruencies:

faith of our fathers, certain music,
and, even now, desire
to take the other's hand, feel
skin. In the Venn diagram

of our lives, more lies outside
the overlap than in. The objects
at the far end of each other's set,
out near the boundary curve,

confuse us still. Perhaps that puzzle
is what sustains us, like geometers
assailing The Happy Ending Problem
to which they will devote their lives.

Miriam Flock first studied poetry with the venerable J.V. Cunningham at Brandeis University. Of her early efforts he said, "It's nice. We won't preserve it, but it's nice." Somehow undeterred, she received her master's in creative writing from Stanford University in 1975, attending workshops with Ken Fields, W.S. Di Piero, and Denise Levertov.

For her day job, Flock taught English and journalism at Santa Clara University, eventually moving into communications. Over the years, her work evolved into a profession as the chief operating officer and communications director of the University's Markkula Center for Applied Ethics. Her articles on ethics appear in many textbooks and journals. Upon her retirement in 2019, she recommitted to her passion for poetry.

Flock's poems have appeared in *Poetry, Georgia Review, Chicago Review,* and *Salmagundi,* among other journals. In 2019, she won the Anna Davidson Rosenberg Award for Poems on the Jewish Experience.

www.ingramcontent.com/pod-product-compliance
Lightning Source LLC
LaVergne TN
LVHW041524070426
835507LV00013B/1811